Message of
Assisi

by
Chris Simpson S.F.O.

All booklets are published thanks to the
generous support of the members of the
Catholic Truth Society

CATHOLIC TRUTH SOCIETY
PUBLISHERS TO THE HOLY SEE

CONTENTS

INTRODUCTION

A visitor to Assisi has a choice of many guide books. Most spend the majority of their pages describing the wonderful art to be found in Assisi. They tend however, to miss the point. Assisi is primarily the place where the most radical Christian of the last 2,000 years lived.

Challenge of St Francis

The first question that one asks is how can a modern tourist town help in understanding the life of a man dedicated to poverty? How can one reconcile Francis' message of simple Gospel living with a rich consumer culture? The answer is twofold. Firstly, underneath the glamour and riches, there are still the buildings and places that St Francis visited. There are the churches he built and the hills upon which he walked. Some things have changed little. Secondly, the contrast between Francis' life and the current European materialism produces a challenge. As people who live within the developed world of the 21st Century, we cannot just run away from it and pretend it does not exist. The challenge for us all is to integrate our spirituality into our current life and world. Assisi may help.

How to meet St Francis

Most of the buildings currently in Assisi were not there during Francis' lifetime. To meet Francis in Assisi you have to suspend your vision of much that is around you. What you have is still a medieval walled city on the foot of Monte Subasio. But you need to imagine, as you look down from the city into the valley, that the entire valley is full of one large forest. This is how it was at the time of Francis. Around the area, there are other towns all of which looked very similar. Spello is only a few kilometres across the hills and in the distance is the hill-town of Perugia. As you walk through the streets, you can still look at the beautiful buildings - and easily ignore the tourists with their cameras on their bus trips and ignore all the motor vehicles. Pretend the gift-shops selling little fat friar eggcups are not there. Imagine that it is still a hustling and bustling town but people are going about their business selling cloth and animals in a noisy market with the Italian temperament to the fore as you hear the locals screaming and shouting. Francis lived in this world. It was a world of violence with wars between towns, crusades and a world of buying and selling. In that sense, it is not too far away from the way we currently live and so the response of Francis is not alien to our modern world.

You may want to discover more about Francis than you can find in this booklet and, if so, you will find further reading on p. 64. I invite you to come on this journey to Assisi to meet Francis. I will start by telling you the story of Francis and I will then take you through the streets to the major sites. Most people stay in Assisi for only a few hours and spend their time in the basilicas. This gives no indication of how Francis lived. This booklet will help you discover Francis over a short trip to Assisi.

THE STORY OF FRANCIS

Before we go into Assisi, it is important that we know about this man, Francis, who changed the history of the Church. He was born in 1182 and died in 1226 in the hilltop town of Assisi in Umbria, between Florence and Rome.

His times

These were hard times. Disease was rampant and life expectancy short. Robbers roamed the city streets and the country paths. There was a feudal system of government based on wealth and war; battles were rife.

The Church was itself one of the wealthiest, and hence most influential, bodies. It was also a major player in the wars. This was the time of the crusades against "the Saracens", the Arabs who had occupied parts of the Mediterranean shores, a time of war between Christians and Muslims.

The Crusades were not the only battles for the people of central Italy. There were Germans in southern Italy who employed Arab mercenaries, there were battles with rich landowners and there were battles with rival cities. For Assisi, the archrival was the city of Perugia across the valley.

His background

Francis was born to a wealthy cloth merchant Pietro Bernadone and his French wife Pica. He was baptised

Giovanni which his father changed to Francesco, meaning little French man, because of his love for France and all things French. His father spent two or three months of the year in France buying cloth, which he would then sell in Umbria. The family lived in the upper part of the town near the central square. The richer you were in Assisi the higher up the hill you would live with the richest and most powerful landowner living in the castle at the top. The rubbish from all the houses was washed down the streets so that the streets lower down the town would be full of the rubbish from those higher up. The air was also considered purer at the top.

Romantic love was greatly revered. The poets and troubadours sang about love and many of their songs had come down from France: the young Francis, with his French mother, would hear these songs constantly. As well as aspiring to find perfect love, these songs also glamorised the role of the soldier. Francis therefore grew up in a materialistic, violent world with dreams of being a knight and winning the love of a great woman.

Military ambitions

As a teenager, he partied in the evenings and was a popular companion to his young friends. He was a born leader and known for his charm and wit as well as being kind and generous. In 1202, at the age of 20, he was able to go into his first battle, a skirmish between Assisi and

Perugia, but he was captured and imprisoned for a year during which time he became very ill, probably as a result of the damp prison conditions. His father purchased his freedom on the grounds of illness and on his return to Assisi Francis remained bedridden. During his illness he began to question his life of parties and making money. This period of Francis' life seemed full of portents and signs for the future. One day a local simpleton put his cloak on the ground in front of Francis indicating that he was going to be great in some way(1)*. On another occasion he met a poor knight and, as he wanted to become a glorious knight, identified closely with him - so the knight gave Francis his own cloak (2). His ambition had not gone and so, spurred on by this, he was excited by another opportunity to become a great knight. This was only fuelled the more by a dream he had of a large palace full of gleaming weapons, shields, chain mail and helmets and a voice proclaiming that they belonged to Francis and his followers (3). So in 1205 he set out to go to Apulia to fight the Germans. The excitement in Assisi must have been intense as Francis and his companions rode out of the city, admired by the whole town, its people cheering them on at the gates. Francis was heading off to become a soldier, a knight and consequently to win his bride.

---

* The numbers in brackets in this chapter refer to the frescos in the Upper Church described on p. 20.

After the first day traveling, the entourage stopped at Spoleto, about 30 miles south of Assisi and here Francis became ill. He heard a voice asking him about the dream of the palace full of arms, saying, "Who do you think will reward you better, the master or his servant?" When Francis answered "The master", the voice said "Then why are you leaving the master for the servant?" On this Francis returned to Assisi, full of humiliation and shattered dreams.

Francis changes

Over the next year, Francis changed. He became more solitary, worked less and started to wander the countryside. He often visited an old, broken-down, derelict church outside Assisi named San Damiano. He was praying and saw the crucifix say to him "Rebuild my church which as you can see is falling into ruin." (4). He took this literally. The challenge of rebuilding a broken down old church inspired Francis and gave him some purpose. It was at this time that he began to live the life of a Penitent. These people, who had given up their roles in society and given themselves to living for the Church, were quite common at the beginning of the 13th century.

Fuelled by the excitement of rebuilding San Damiano, Francis sold some of his father's cloth to buy stones. Unfortunately, his father Pietro saw this as the last straw. His son had not only failed to go to battle, but had been sickly, had not been working hard, and was now selling his cloth to build a church. His father asked for the money back. Francis refused and Pietro took his son to court. As Francis was a Penitent, he did not accept the authority of the civil courts and insisted that the Bishop try the case. This led to a confrontation between Pietro and Francis at the Bishop's Palace.

This event would have caused a great scandal and the townsfolk must have gathered around to hear the Bishop's verdict. The Bishop sided with Pietro at which Francis, in a most dramatic gesture, removed all of his own clothes in public, stood naked in front of the Bishop and his father and said to his father, "From now on it is not my father Pietro Bernadone but, my Father who art in Heaven" and saying this returned all his clothes to his father (5). He then walked out of the city naked.

His new life

Francis lived outside the city walls in the forest and began to beg for stones. He was treated with contempt by the people of Assisi but he was not discouraged and continued to rebuild San Damiano, as he knew this was the mission given him by God.

This new life of Francis challenged all in Assisi. Their lives revolved around wars, battles, money and, for his friends, parties and fun. He had rejected this to live a life of poverty, he was begging for food and stones and building up a broken down church. Nevertheless, he appeared happy and content with his new life.

After rebuilding San Damiano, he moved on to another derelict chapel nearby, Santa Maria Degli Angeli. He went to Mass there regularly and in 1208, he heard the tenth chapter of St Matthew's Gospel in which Christ spoke to his apostles sending them into the world. They are urged to go "proclaiming that the Kingdom of Heaven is close at hand." "Cure the sick, raise the dead, cleanse the lepers, and cast out devils". In particular, it says, "you received without charge, give without charge. Provide yourselves with no gold or silver, not even with a few coppers for your purses, with no haversack for the journey or spare tunic or footwear or a staff, for the workman deserves his keep." Francis knew immediately that this was Christ speaking to him. This would be his life. It would be dedicated to Christ's peace and love, living in poverty and seeing God in all things around him. He would be a knight for Christ. He had found his bride whom he called Lady Poverty.

Living the Gospel

He put on an old tunic of the type the hill farmers used and wore no shoes. He must have been surprised when others came to join him, especially some of his old friends. As his way of life had attracted new adherents he began to think that he needed to seek the approval of the Church. When there were 12 brothers living according to

St Francis' inspiration, they decided to travel to Rome to
see the Pope to obtain approval for their new way of life.
Amazingly, the Pope, after having a dream about Francis
holding up the Lateran palace from collapsing, agreed to
see this scruffy man and his friends (6). Francis's rule
was based on Christ's instructions to his apostles from St
Matthew's Gospel. The Pope could hardly disagree and
gave approval to this new way of living (7).

St Clare

Others came to join him. A young girl from Assisi, Clare,
who had observed the transformation of the heroic, party-
going soldier to a ragged beggar living for Christ, joined
him in the forest outside Assisi on Palm Sunday evening in
1212. Clare was also from the upper part of the city but
was a few years younger than Francis. She had started
giving money away to the poor and had earlier in the year
discussed her plans with Francis. All was carefully planned
as Clare sneaked out of her house at night and came down
the valley escorted by friends to the Portiuncula. Francis
and his companions were waiting. She was led into the
church and exchanged her elegant dress for a simple habit
and then made the vows of penitence and obedience
required for joining Francis's order. He then symbolically
cut off her hair. Clare had not come to the Portiuncula to
become a conventional nun but to work like Francis for
those in need. However, she could not stay at the

Portiuncula with the men as she knew her family would come to take her away. Francis therefore had organised for her to go to a nearby convent for a while. Her family was furious and tried to bring her back to Assisi but failed. She moved to another convent and eventually the Bishop gave Clare San Damiano and the little house next to it. By then Clare's sister Catherine and her mother's cousin Pacifica had also joined her. They made their Franciscan vows and became part of the Franciscan order. The order grew quickly as a form of a movement inspired by Clare. Initially there was no official rule, just 'constitutions' laid down by the church. Clare wrote the Rule in 1253, and in 1263 the movement's official name was pronounced as 'The Order of St Clare'. They are also known as the Poor Clares or Second Order of St Francis.

The Third Order of St Francis, or Secular Franciscans, were those attracted to the life of Francis but who wished to remain within the world. They were seen at the time as being Franciscan Penitents. The first order of Francis, the Friars Minor, were those men who joined Francis in the forest.

Francis preaching

Francis and his companions went about in pairs proclaiming "that the kingdom of heaven is close at hand." They followed Christ's instructions to the apostles and began traveling throughout Italy and then into

Europe. There are many stories about Francis and his friars. On one occasion Francis' friars saw a vision of him in a fiery chariot in the sky when he was in fact praying in a secluded place (8). On another occasion, a friar had a vision of heaven where he saw a throne reserved for the humble Francis (9). Once he ordered one of his friars to cast out devils from Arezzo, a nearby town, as there were many wicked people living there (10). He was seen levitating (12) and bilocating (being in two places at once - he once appeared to a Franciscan chapter in Arles) (18). One story tells of how he was asked round to dinner at a knights' house and during the dinner the knight became a Christian and confessed his sins. That same evening his host suddenly died (16). Although some of the stories appear far-fetched, they give an indication of the kind of man Francis was and the amazing influence and popularity he received during his lifetime. He was even asked to preach to the Pope (17). The numbers of the Friars Minor grew, as did the Poor Clares and Secular Franciscans.

Peacemaker

He also saw a role in bringing peace in disputes between people and countries. In a remarkable act of peacemaking, he went to Egypt to meet the Sultan Malik-al-Kamil in 1219. Instead of fighting as a knight in the Crusades, he went to the enemy to attempt to bring peace through dialogue. He hoped for martyrdom and his strategy for peace was to convert the Sultan to Christianity. Francis challenged the Sultan's priests to walk through fire to show their faith but, whilst he did it, they declined (11). He did this to repair and make up for his Christian forebears who had refused such a challenge from Muhammad at Medina. During the days of discussion between the Sultan and Francis, they developed a mutual respect for each other. Although the Sultan could not give up his religion and hence his throne and life, he developed an admiration for Francis' simplicity and fervour. The two leading lights from these great religions saw God in each other. In this meeting with the Sultan we see how Francis had changed from the war-mongering soldier to the peace-loving prophet.

Nature and Poverty

He saw Christ in all of nature around him. This was not just an admiration of its beauty but the recognition that it was from God. He said he could see the fingerprint of Christ in every leaf and when asked about the weather he would say, "the weather is always beautiful, it is just different." In the famous story of preaching to the birds (15), he was encouraging them to praise God with their singing and flying.

Francis saw poverty as being close to Christ, he saw the King of the world being born in a stable in poverty and dying a criminal's death on a cross. For him to be close to

Christ was to be in poverty. He loathed seeing other poor people and always wanted to be poorer than them. A story tells of how he gave away his ragged tunic on numerous occasions and another one tells of how, following praying, a spring developed from the ground to quench the thirst of a poor man (14). He loved the nativity and re-enacted it with a real baby in Greccio (13) one Christmas - this began the tradition of the Christmas crib.

The stigmata

Francis considered that all pain and suffering brought him closer to Christ. In 1224 whilst praying on Mount La Verna, a six-winged seraph with the five wounds of Christ appeared to Francis. Francis developed wounds in his hands, feet and side similar to Christ - this was the first ever case of stigmata (19). The stigmata in his feet changed his skin into the shape of a nail protruding from his sole. Walking was painful and so he wore sandals, hence the Franciscan tradition of wearing sandals. The stigmata remained with him until he died. They bled and were painful. For Francis this was the ultimate way of being close to Christ: he shared the pain with Christ as part of his identification with, and love for Him.

His legacy

Francis died in Assisi in 1226 (20). Tradition has it that one of his brothers in the south of Italy who was mute and dying shouted out "Wait for me Francis, I'm coming with you" as Francis died (21). After he died, his stigmata were carefully studied and authenticated (22) and his body was taken past the grieving Poor Clares (23). Following his death there were many reported miracles including a man being cured after praying to Francis (26), a woman dying and being brought back to life so as to confess a mortal sin (27) and the miraculous release from prison of a repentant heretic (28). At one point the Pope had some doubts about the stigmata but Francis appeared to him in a dream and filled a vial full of blood from the would on his side (25). He was canonised only two years after he died (24).

By listening to Christ, he had begun to rebuild his Church. He had done this by living a radical life in which he took Christ's words literally and, as Christ had done before him, turned upside down the world view of wealth and power. The Holy Spirit led this remarkable man to be so close to Christ that he developed the wounds of, and suffered with, Christ.

BASILICA DI SAN FRANCESCO

As you arrive in Assisi, the most striking site is the protruding Basilica and convent of Francis. It is best approached from the car park. Walk through the narrow streets, ignore the gift shops, and remember how Francis walked through these same streets.

Francis would be shocked at the grandeur of the Basilica. He lived a simple life of prayer and praising God but when he died at the age of 44 years there was a risk that his body would be stolen. He had already been acclaimed as a living saint during his lifetime and had followers throughout Europe. In those times, relics of the saints were highly sought after. Perugia for one would be wishing to steal his body to put in their town in the belief that it would protect their city. Assisi, and the Friars who took over the running of the Franciscan order, could not allow his body to be stolen. Therefore, even though Francis had never believed in owning buildings, which would require him to protect them, the friars had his body put in a tomb surrounded by stone slabs and metal bars. On top of this was built a large cathedral to protect it. Work on the construction of the Basilica began in 1128, only 2 years after the death of Francis. Some rich citizens of the city gave the rocky terrain at the edge of the town to the Pope in trust for the Franciscan order. It was the area of the town where executions took place. Brother Elias had taken over the running of the order and it is thought that he might have been the architect. The lower church was completed within two years. As Francis was so acclaimed the cathedral had to be magnificent and large. The greatest artists of the time were commissioned to decorate it. These paintings were not just for beauty but also to tell the story of Francis to a mainly illiterate population.

The Basilica is in the shape of a Tau cross. This is a cross in the shape of a 'T', which has become a special sign of Francis. Its origins lie in the Old Testament when the Prophet Ezekiel (9:4) uses the imagery of the last letter of the alphabet in asking Israel to remain faithful to God until the end and to be "sealed" with the mark of the Tau on their foreheads. For Christians the Tau came to represent the Cross of Crucifixion. Then the religious community of Anthony the Hermit, for whom Francis worked after his conversion, used the Tau to protect the lepers with whom they worked. Francis adopted it, so it symbolised for him fidelity to the Church, the Crucifixion and service to the outcast of the day. Now you will see the Tau throughout Assisi.

In September 1997 an earthquake damaged large parts of Assisi, the consequences of which can still be seen. You may recall images of the ceiling of the Upper Basilica crashing down on people!

The Upper Church

The Basilica consists of Francis' tomb, on top of which is the Lower Church and then, above this, is the Upper Church. The Upper Church is where the roof crashed down during the earthquake.

Significant in the Upper Church are the Frescos, painted by the greatest painter of his age, Giotto di Bondone, who is widely considered to be the first artist of the Renaissance and the frescoes are his earliest known works. Giotto spent two periods of time in Assisi. In 1282, when he was about 25 years old, he painted some frescos near the altar. He then returned for two years in 1297 to portray the life of Francis in 28 frescos based on the biography by Thomas of Celano which was drawn from the oral tradition and from accounts of people who had known the saint personally. They tell the story of Francis for the illiterate people of the time. It is worth noting that Francis changed the way people saw the world. He was the first to see God's work in all that is around us. He saw the fingerprints of God on every leaf and the beauty of every animal as God had created them all.

This changed art. Prior to this time art concentrated on characters and what they were doing. Following Francis, pictures showed beautiful scenery and were much brighter. It is like the change from black and white television to colour, but the reason was that the colour showed us God's beautiful world.

This is where to find the basic story of Francis. In Britain and North America Francis is famous for preaching to the birds. He certainly did do this but Italians see him more as the man who lived in poverty and received the stigmata. He was also the man that started three major religious orders. In some ways the story of Francis was romantic and poetic, as portrayed in Zefferelli's film 'Brother Sun, Sister Moon'. In other ways it was harsh and rugged; he lived a life owning nothing, wearing little and accepting the harsh conditions of Italian weather and illnesses such as tuberculosis from which he died.

The stories behind each of the frescos are told in the previous chapter. It is nice to walk around them in order to see the whole story of Francis unfold. The first one is to the right of the main altar as you look up the nave.

1. Francis honoured by a fellow citizen
2. Francis gives away his cloak
3. Dream of the palace filled with weapons
4. Francis before the crucifix of San Damiano
5. Renunciation of his inheritance and earthly possessions
6. The dream of Pope Innocent III
7. The approval of the rule
8. The vision of the fiery chariot
9. The vision of the thrones in heaven

There are innumerable stories about Francis and these give just a flavour. They can come across as a little too simplistic. Try to remember the harshness of the life he lived. He was down in the valley in those woods as it rained and snowed. He went about with his friars praising God and preaching.

Before leaving this area, it is worth a visit to the shop between the Upper and Lower Basilica. As you go down the steps at the far end of the Upper Church you come to the shop. If you want to buy anything in Assisi, this is about the best place. It is inexpensive and run by the Franciscans.

The Lower Church

After leaving the shop, there are steps down to the Lower Church. Before going down the steps, look up. There is a feint fresco of Jesus carrying the cross and looking back to see, a few metres behind, Francis carrying his cross. Then go down the steps.

The Lower Church is dark and full of paintings and frescoes. These were painted to honour the saint and tell his story. Assisi has become popular for art lovers but it is far too easy to concentrate on the frescoes and miss the point of Francis. If you only wanted to see one fresco in the Lower Church then I would draw your attention to the Three Allegories and Francis in Glory above the Altar. The allegories are of obedience (the yoke around Francis' neck), chastity (symbolised by a maiden clothed in white) and poverty (whereby St Francis is marrying Lady Poverty.)

The most important part of the Lower Basilica are the relics of St Francis in the Cappella delle Relique di San Francesco. This is in a small chapel in one of the transepts off the main altar. It is easily missed but it is a must. On seeing the relics of Francis you are confronted with the reality of this man. In particular, his habit is coarse, rough, and full of patches. It is possible to see how this is the prototype for the modern friars' habits, which are somewhat smarter nowadays. Other relics on display are a soft piece of leather used for covering his wounds, a blessing he wrote on a piece of paper to one of his friends and a pair of his sandals. Seeing these relics confronts us with what Francis was really like and how harsh life must have been.

The Tomb of St Francis

It is difficult to explain why but this is one of the holiest places in the world. Francis is buried in a tomb surrounded by slabs of stone held in place by metal bars. This is above the altar. His body is here. They opened the coffin in 1978 and found the bones of a man in his 40's who had tuberculosis in his spine. The atmosphere is charged. Millions of people experience the same thing here; a place of peace and intense spirituality. Unfortunately, it is always busy in the summer and if you can, it is advisable to visit first thing in the morning. Masses start at about 6.30am and it really is worth getting up early. Around the side of the tomb are the burial places of Francis' four closest companions, Leo, Masseo, Angelo and Rufino. Spend some time here in prayer.

There is a fantastic little book called the 'Small Miracle' by Paul Gallico about Francis' tomb. It tells of a

little orphan boy from Assisi who owns a donkey. When
the donkey becomes ill, the boy believes that the only
way to cure him is to take him down to the tomb but the
donkey cannot get down the steps. The boy's faith and
determination are immense; he will not give up hope even
when the Church does not initially appear to support him.
Without giving anything of the story away, you can see
that the inspiration of Francis shines through.

The tomb of St Francis.

SAN DAMIANO

San Damiano was the little church that Francis rebuilt. It is only 1.5 kilometres outside the walls of Assisi. Remember that this was in the woods at the time of Francis, so as you walk down the path towards San Damiano imagine being surrounded by a forest and then coming across an old derelict chapel.

After he restored the chapel, it was further developed into the first Poor Clare convent. St Clare wanted to live a life of poverty and simplicity, but was unable to wander through the countryside with the friars, as this would have been unacceptable in the 13th Century. However, she was able to live a contemplative life of prayer with other women and where better than at the place where Francis had started his building work. Nowadays San Damiano is a house for a community of Franciscan friars.

A visit to San Damiano is therefore in two stages, the chapel and the first Poor Clare Convent.

The Chapel

The chapel, together with Francis' tomb, is one of the most inspiring places in the world. It is best visited first thing in the morning and the 7.15am Mass is wonderful. I have often been early in the morning; on entering the chapel before the Mass, it all looks dark. As my eyes begin to get used to the darkness I can see figures in the pews. It then becomes apparent that the chapel is full of people silently praying, some in the pews and some just kneeling on the floor. It has become a favourite place for young adults to congregate and pray. These are the people who are often the true pilgrims to Assisi. They are trying to discover their own role in our busy materialistic world and, like Francis, are praying in this chapel waiting for God's word.

It is good to go into the chapel, go into a pew and kneel down next to the wall. Touch the stones. These are the stones that Francis and his friends actually laid. Imagine in the dark the old broken-down church and see the crucifix in front of you. This is not the original that spoke to Francis but a replica (the original is in the Basilica of Santa Chiara). Be still and wait to hear what God wants to say to you.

The Convent

Once you have finished this, it is time to go on the next stage of the visit to San Damiano. Unfortunately there are strict opening times to enter the rest of the building and it is not possible after the 7.15am mass. So check the times before you visit. If you walk past the tabernacle, there is an exit on the right that leads you into the old Poor Clare convent. You will walk through the choir stalls and go up some stairs. Half way up the stairs on the right is a terrace. It was on this terrace that Francis wrote the poem

'Canticle of the Creatures'. He was staying here with the Poor Clares when ill and looked out over the valley and wrote his praises of God through nature. This was quite novel at the time and was an early expression of our seeing God's work through his creation. Francis used to see himself as part of all creation and therefore similar to the animals, the trees and flowers and the sun and the moon. He referred to them all as brother or sister so that there was his Father in heaven and he was one of the creatures with his brothers and sisters.

Carry on up the stairs and you will reach Clare's Dormitory. This is a large bare room with a cross marking the place where Clare died, aged 60 years, in 1253. There is a door in this room that opens onto the front of the church. In 1241, Assisi escaped invasion by the Saracens. As they came towards Assisi, Clare opened this door and held up the Blessed Sacrament. The brilliance of the light, which came from the Sacred Host repelled the army.

The tour takes you downstairs into a beautiful, peaceful cloister. Walk around it and you will come across the refectory where Clare's nuns ate their meals.

BASILICA DI SANTA CHIARA

If you walk back up to Assisi from San Damiano this Basilica is just inside the walls. It is not an exceptionally attractive church, but within it there are some extraordinary sites.

As you enter, go straight down the knave and turn right into the Chapel of the Crucifix of San Damiano. Inside is the original crucifix, a 12th century icon painted by a Syrian monk, which used to hang in San Damiano and which spoke to Francis telling him to rebuild the church. It is inspired by St John's gospel but little is known about its history. All we know is that it ended up in an old church in the forest outside Assisi. No one thought much about it as the wind and rain weathered the old wood but it was this simple crucifix, left for ruin, that spoke to Francis and changed his life. It is a typical story of Francis: He heard the words "Francis, go, repair my house, which, as you see, is falling into ruin". Nowadays we see the full meaning of these words but Francis just took them literally, he went out, bought the stones, and started to rebuild San Damiano. Take a while to kneel down and pray, as Francis did, to see what God wants you to do.

Beyond the crucifix is another chapel and on the right you will see a grill. The Poor Clare nuns pray behind this. If you arrive at the time of their office then you can pray with them as their voices are relayed through a microphone so that, although you cannot see them, you can hear them.

After leaving this chapel there is a sign which leads down into the crypt where the tomb of Clare lies. At the bottom of the stairs go left and you will see relics of St Clare.

Clare is often depicted as a beautiful young woman. She had the same vision as Francis in seeing the emptiness of the struggle to obtain more wealth and the need to give up possessions and to live a life of poverty in order to grow closer to Christ. They would both describe how Christ came into the world in complete poverty in a stable in Bethlehem as a sign for the world of the uselessness of money. To be close to Christ we have to reject all worldly wealth. As Clare left her family and came down the valley to meet Francis in the forest, it is believed that he symbolically cut her hair and put a shawl over her head. The long golden hair in Santa Chiara may have been the hair cut off by Francis.

After seeing the relics you can go to the tomb of Clare on the other side of the crypt.

PIAZZA DEL COMUNE AND THE STREETS OF ASSISI

Piazza del Comune is the centre of Assisi. It divides Assisi into two; everything below here is described as *Sotto* and everything above is *Sopra*. In medieval times, these two areas were quite distinct and characterised by competition between them. *Sopra* was the richer area and *Sotto* the poorer. This rivalry is commemorated each year by a festival starting the first Thursday in May called *Calendimaggio*. It is a wonderful, colourful festival which lasts for three days and is well worth a visit. There is marching, singing and the town is lit up with burning torches. The participants dress in bright medieval costumes and take part in medieval pursuits like jousting. The largest competitions take place in Piazza del Comune as the groups from *Sotto* and *Sopra* meet. It is one big party and a reminder of the life of Francis before his conversion.

Calendimaggio aside, Piazza del Comune is a great central square. Not many of the buildings would have been present at the time of Francis except for the old Roman Temple of Minerva. The first Giotto fresco, which we saw in the Basilica di San Francesco, shows it clearly.

The best thing to do in Piazza del Comune is to sit down and watch people go by. This is a good Italian pastime and it is easy to sit around for a few hours and do absolutely nothing except look at people. It is useful to do this in one of the cafes that have tables out in the square whilst drinking a cappuccino, but for those unable or unwilling to pay for such luxuries, there are the steps of the temple or the steps around the fountain. Just be Italian! See the people go by and then imagine life at the time of Francis. The tourists would not be there, but there would still be the people rushing around from one place to another selling things. At one time Francis would have been one of them but later on, he would become the rather odd little man in the brown habit walking through the streets singing or begging for food or stones. Francis is still here.

Most people walk through the streets below Piazza del Comune in the *Sotto* region. I much prefer the streets above Piazza del Comune. I support *Sopra* at *Calendimaggio* but you have to walk up the hill to get there. It is well worth the trip and as you go further up you will come across picturesque little streets in which the local people still live. This is where to find interesting restaurants and cheaper places to stay. Apart from the streets, two other sites may be worth a quick visit. The Cattedrale di San Rufino is the cathedral of the town and certainly looks nice from the outside. It is at the end of a lovely rectangular Piazza above which there is a nice coffee chop with chairs outside in the summer; a good place to take a rest. The beautiful façade is Romanesque. Inside there are old paintings and statues although none have any major significance in the story of Francis.

The other site that some people like to see is the castle at the top of the hill. This is referred to as the Rocca. It is a typical ruined castle and was built in 1367, nearly a hundred years after St Francis died. However on this site, before the current building, was another castle which was lived in by a tyrant. In 1198 the people of Assisi rebelled against him and the fortress was captured and destroyed. Francis was then 16 years old and likely to have been involved in the battle. Nevertheless, standing on the Rocca provides magnificent views around Assisi and of the hills behind. I always imagine Francis wandering through the hills with his Friars singing and laughing. In addition, for those who are interested in the film 'Brother Sun, Sister Moon' by Zefferelli, the Rocca was used for quite a few of the scenes. If you know the film, you will recognise some of the inside areas where they built false floors for the film.

The Sotto region below Piazza Del Comune is much easier to walk around as it is downhill, but is more spoilt and more commercialised than the upper part of the town. One of the nicest roads is Via Bernardo De Quintavalle where the house of Bernard of Quintavalle lies. Bernard was a friend of Francis and was the first to join him in the wood. Although all you now see is an old house, it is nice to imagine Francis coming round to Bernard's house for a meal and trying to explain why he had given up the family business, stripped naked, left the city and was wandering around in peasants clothes begging for stones. After the meal, Francis was invited to stay the night and while Bernard pretended to be asleep, he heard Francis praying repeatedly "my God and my all". It must have taken a lot of courage for Bernard to go and join the 'mad man Francis' down in the valley.

SANTA MARIA DEGLI ANGELI

The second church that Francis began to rebuild was the church of Santa Maria degli Angeli which was surrounded by an area called the Portiuncula or 'little portion' of land. It was here that Francis was attending Mass one day and working out what he should be doing in his life. Up until then he had just been rebuilding churches, but he heard in the Gospel that Christ's disciples should "provide yourselves with no gold or silver not even with a few coppers for your purses, with no haversack for the journey or spare tunic or footwear or a staff, for the workman deserves his keep" (*Mt* 10:9-10). On hearing this, Francis based the rule of his order upon it and chose his way of life.

A massive cathedral in the valley below Assisi now surrounds the Chapel of the Portiuncula. The Basilica of Santa Maria degli Angeli has a Renaissance style façade which was built in 1927 after an earthquake had damaged its predecessor. The church itself has nothing to particularly recommend it apart from the gem within it, the original tiny chapel of the Portiuncula. Go into the chapel, kneel by the walls so as to touch the stones that Francis placed there, close your eyes and imagine you are in a little chapel in the middle of a forest. Surprisingly this is the chapel where it all began, and from where the enormous Franciscan Order originates.

The effect of Francis on society at the time was striking, with his spirituality engulfing the church and the world as people flocked to join him. It is also interesting to look around now to see the effect of this little place. One of them is that Los Angeles was named after it as Franciscans went to the West Coast of America. Of course, San Francisco was similarly named after Francis.

At the time of Francis, there were little huts around the Portiuncula where the friars would sleep. They never owned any of their buildings but were allowed to borrow them from others.

After leaving the chapel of the Portiuncula there is a place, to the right whilst facing the high altar, where Francis died in one of the huts. Just nearby is a passageway that leads round to some ruins of earlier monasteries and past a rose garden where the roses have no thorns. Francis threw himself into the roses after sinning and the thorns miraculously vanished. Continue along the passageway as it also leads to the souvenir shop, which is in fact the best in the area. It is less expensive than most and actually has some reasonably nice things to buy if you want to spend any money. Again, as at the Basilica di San Francesco, you can buy souvenirs at a reasonable price as it is run by the friars.

THE CARCERI AND THE HILLS OF MONTE SUBASIO

After the activity and noise of Assisi, it is refreshing to get out to a place of retreat. The Carceri, which is Italian for prison, is where Francis used to go to get away. Francis was, like many saints, a preacher who required long periods of solitude to get close to God. He had elements of the evangelist and the hermit. He had a number of quiet retreat places but the Carceri was his favourite. It is 4km from Assisi, up the hill, half way up Monte Subasio. If you are athletic, it is well worth the walk but otherwise it is a hire car or taxi journey.

Francis has a peculiar effect on people so let me give you a warning. When I lived in Assisi I helped a disabled friar who offered me any treat that I would like. My choice was to stay at the Carceri for a week in the little Friary. I chose to walk there but to show my commitment to poverty and closeness to Francis I chose to walk without shoes. This seemed a fantastic idea at the time! My delicate middle class pink feet were not in a hardened state to cope with the asphalt roads. I ended up in absolute agony at the Carceri with blisters on the soles of my feet. This pain did not ruin my time there and in a strange way made me feel closer to the spirit of Francis. It is a great walk but I would suggest you keep your shoes on!

The Carceri at the time of Francis consisted of a few caves and huts in a wood. Nowadays a Friary has been built but it remains a very tranquil, beautiful place. Within the Friary, you can see where Francis used to hide away and pray and outside in the woods you can explore, through the paths, his friends' hideaways which were caves in the rocks. The woods are beautiful and you cannot fail to be grateful to God for the beauty of his creation.

After visiting the Carceri it is well worth a trip to the top of Monte Subasio if you are in a car. It is quite a large hill but it is wonderfully barren and wind-swept at the top above the tree line. Don't stay in the car but get out and walk around a little and imagine a couple of ragged men, bare foot in old brown habits singing and laughing as they walk through the hills.

OTHER PLACES TO VISIT

Church of San Stefano

This is situated just off the main road between Piazza Comune and the Basilica Di San Francesco and is a lovely little old church. It is not a place where tourists go and is a little retreat inside Assisi. Its only claim to fame in the story of Francis is that on his death the bells began to ring spontaneously.

Rivo Torto

Rivo Torto is down in the valley beyond Santa Maria Degli Angeli. It is one of the earlier places where Francis and his ragged band of men used to live. It was an old shelter but Francis was eventually ejected, as the owner needed it for his animals. Unfortunately, the original buildings have been destroyed, so a replica has been rebuilt within a church. This rather loses the magic of the place and it is only worth a visit if you are in the area for quite a few days.

Santa Maria Maggiore

This church, which is just below the Basilica Di Santa Chiara, is of interest as it used to be the Cathedral of Assisi at the time of Francis. It was rebuilt after a fire between 1212 and 1228, which was at the time of Francis' life. Next to the church is the bishop's palace, which has been rebuilt and in fact would have been the site of Francis' trial by his father and where Francis stripped off his clothes to leave the town.

Chiesa Nuova

This church is situated just near Piazza del Comune and was built in 1616 and thought to be on the site of the house of Francis' father Pietro Bernardone. Inside you can see the entrance doorway and part of the shop where Francis helped his father. There is also what appears to be a cell that was probably part of the basement where Francis was locked up by his father when he was behaving in ways which his father disapproved. There were many problems between Pietro and Francis, as Pietro could not understand why Francis would want to give things away and spend so long praying. He was beaten and put in this cell on occasions.

Down the little street from here is a small chapel called Francesco Piccolino. This is a place where Francis was supposed to have been born, although the story is unlikely to be true. The legend is that his mother was frightened when she was giving birth to him and asked to be taken to the stable to feel closer to Joseph and Mary. Although he is unlikely to have been born in the stable, there is evidence that this was, in fact, the site of his father's house, not at Chiesa Nuova. The stables were all below the houses and the front door was above the stable. A ladder was let down during the day and pulled up at night for security.

A Life of Simplicity

How was it that this little poor man of Assisi became so incredibly popular in his lifetime and remains one of the most popular and influential people of the last 2,000 years? At one level, he was just a man who had his own vision of how to live a life for Christ and left the world in which he lived, initially for a life in the midst of nature, and then wandering around the countryside preaching. He lived the Gospel. He responded directly to the call to live simply. On one occasion soon after his conversion he prayed for guidance and opened the Gospels in three places. The first was "If you wish to be perfect, go and sell what you own and give the money to the poor" (*Mt* 19:21). The second was "Take nothing for the journey: neither staff nor haversack nor bread nor money" (*Lk* 9:3). The final reading was "If anyone wants to be a follower of mine let him renounce himself and take up his cross and follow me" (*Mt* 16:24). He was completely Gospel centred - he lived it. The surprise to him must have been that other people were attracted to the same idea and followed him. He did not start out to form a religious order; he just wanted to live the Gospel. At another level, he was rejecting the preoccupations of central European culture at that time; these were to do with commerce, making wars with neighbouring towns or crusades against

Muslims. He was also rejecting his previous party-going life style. This is therefore not too different to the world of today and gives us a hint of why he remains so popular. 21st century European and North American culture is also preoccupied with commerce and making wars. Others, through the centuries, have been attracted to going out into the woods, by leaving the preoccupations of the world for a life following the Gospels.

Three elements of Francis help to clarify his approach to life. These can be seen as Francis would have seen them or as the 21st century Franciscan sees them

1 Seeing Christ in Nature

He was the first to see God working through the plants, the trees, the animals and other people; all of these show the glory of God and should be celebrated. "God saw all he had made, and indeed it was very good." (*Ge* 1:31) On one occasion when a wolf was roaming the forest outside the city of Gubbio he went directly to the wolf whom he greeted in the name of Christ. He organised for the locals to leave food for the wolf in return for leaving the townsfolk alone. He preached to the birds telling them to praise God. He avoided walking on insects. If he saw twigs or plants in the shape of a cross he would stop and pray. He used to say "The weather is always beautiful, it is just different." He was not in a world where environmental destruction was occurring but it is clear from his views on the world that such global destruction would nowadays have called him to action. He would want us to respect the beauty that God has given us. He would echo Pope John Paul II's words "Man is no longer the Creator's steward, but an autonomous despot, who is finally beginning to understand that he must stop at the edge of the abyss".

2 Love of Poverty

Francis saw Christ as the ultimate man of poverty. He was preoccupied by how Christ, who owned everything, chose to be born in a stable. Francis aimed to be so poor so that he could identify with Christ but as part of this he did not want anyone else to be poorer than himself. If he came across anyone poorer he would insist on giving away some of his clothes to them. Poverty then becomes something to be achieved to be close to Christ and to understand the plight of the poor in the world. "How happy are the poor in spirit, theirs is the Kingdom of heaven" (*Mt* 5:3). He emphasised to his followers the importance of not owning things and therefore not being attached to them. God would provide "Think of the flowers; they never have to spin or weave: yet, I assure you, not even Solomon in all his regalia was robed like one of these." (*Lk* 12:27) He saw Lady Poverty as his bride. The lack of possessions is to stand shoulder to shoulder with Christ and the poor. Once when asked by the Bishop why the friars could not grow their own food on their own land he replied "Possessions are often the cause of disputes and often violence. If we owned them we would be obliged to carry arms to defend them - and to do that would hinder us in loving God and our neighbour." The story of True and Perfect Joy shows how he always wanted to be below everyone.

3 Striving for Peace

Francis worked endlessly for peace at the interpersonal level, so that he would intervene to help resolve arguments, and also at the international level. "Happy the peacemakers: they shall be called sons of God" (*Mt* 5:9). As a young man, Francis wanted to join the crusades but after his conversion, he ended up going to the East to meet a Sultan. His aim was to stop the fighting through dialogue. Imagine this now: two nations at war and a little poor man goes and meets the head of state of the other country and they discuss peace. Followers of Francis throughout the centuries have continued to use peaceful means to try to resolve conflicts. It is no coincidence that John Paul II twice called leaders of all the world religions to Assisi to pray for peace.

These three themes are underpinned by a simplicity which is characteristic of Francis. He never looked for the complicated deeper meaning but when he heard the crucifix speak at San Damiano or read the Gospel saying

John Paul II prays for Peace outside the Basilica of Assisi with the Religious Leaders from around the world.

what Christ's disciples should do, he took them literally and acted. Similarly, his life was based on simplicity reflecting Meister Eckhart's philosophy that spirituality is about subtraction not addition, that is the more we take away the closer we get to God.

These Franciscan ideas can all be seen within the modern Assisi. Most striking are the good and holy people who regularly come to Assisi to develop their life to face the pressures of the modern world. After staying in Assisi awhile and pondering on the stories of Francis, we see the world in different ways. I recall when I lived there meeting a group of 19 year-olds who had hitched to Assisi. They came to stay where I was working and I met and prayed with them. One of them had written on the back of his jacket "everything I own belongs to you" and he was determined to live a life of poverty sharing everything with others. He had no shoes and had no money to buy them. I was collecting my drying from the washing line one day and found attached to my t-shirt a $5 note. I could not work out how this had arrived in the private garden where I dried my clothes. Everyone who had access to the garden denied any knowledge and I had to conclude that either someone had sneaked in and put a $5 note on my clothes or it had materialised from nowhere. Within the spiritual environment of Assisi, it was clear that the $5 was from God and so the question was what to do about it. That evening whilst praying with my friends the one with no shoes prayed that somehow he could get some sandals as his feet were hurting. It was clear that the $5 was for him and indeed was exactly the right amount to buy some cheap sandals. That is what Assisi is about. People living radical lifestyles and knowing that Christ will look after them.

Assisi has affected the world over the past 800 years. The naming of major cities, the use of cribs at Christmas and even the tradition of the Stations of the Cross is Franciscan. The Pope held peace meetings in Assisi in 1986 and most recently in 2002. Franciscans have taken the Christian message to all corners of the world and, wherever one lives, the site of the brown habit and cord is visible today. The three orders continue to flourish throughout the world with the friars in most countries. The Poor Clares have convents throughout the world but are not visible. Once you know of their existence you can find them. There are two convents within a 40-mile radius of where I live. The Secular Franciscans are the lay people who are living normal lives throughout the world and have pledged themselves to live a Gospel life according to the way of Francis. There are estimated to be over one million of these but again they are not too noticeable. They do not wear a habit and just go about doing their normal work in the world inspired by Francis' example.

The effect of St Francis on people's lives can be seen by looking at how lifestyles are changed by the millions of people throughout the world who want to live a Franciscan life. They do not all give up their possessions but they do learn how not to be attached to them. They seek to respect the environment in which they live and they work for peace in their personal lives and in the larger community. The saints who have taken up this challenge speak for themselves. St Margaret of Cortona lived as a mistress to an important man and bore an illegitimate child and then, after her lover's death, became a Secular Franciscan. Dante was a Secular Franciscan. St Maximilian Kolbe was a Franciscan friar who in Auschwitz prayed with the prisoners before offering to replace a married man for torture and death. John Bradburne was a Secular Franciscan who was martyred in Zimbabwe during the revolution in 1979 for his work in helping the poor lepers of the area. Fr Mychal Judge was the 68 year old Franciscan friar and chaplain to the New York Fire Department. His was the first body to be recovered after the Twin Towers terrorist attack in September 2001. "Fr Mike" had gone to help after hearing of the first aircraft hitting the World Trade Centre. A piece of debris struck him as he was administering the last rites to a fireman.

The last 800 years have inspired so many to live a radical Gospel-centred life.

Prayers and Readings for the Pilgrim

Canticle of the Creatures

Most High, all-powerful, good Lord,
Yours are the praises the glory, and the honour,
  and all blessing
To You alone, Most High, do they belong,
And no human is worthy to mention Your name.
Praise be you, my Lord, with all Your creatures
Especially Sir Brother Sun,
Who is the day and through whom You give us light.
And he is Beautiful and radiant with great splendour;
And bears a likeness of You, Most High One.
Praised be You, my Lord,
  through Sister Moon and the stars,
In heaven You formed them
  clear and precious and beautiful.
Praised be You, my Lord, through Brother Wind,
And through the air, cloudy and serene,
  and every kind of weather,
Through whom You give sustenance
  to Your creatures.
Praised be You, my Lord through Sister Water,
Who is very useful and humble
  and precious and chaste.

Praised be You, my Lord, through Brother Fire,
Through whom You light the night,
And he is beautiful and playful and robust and strong.
Praised be You, my Lord,
  through our Sister Mother Earth,
Who sustains and governs us,
And who produces various fruit
  with coloured flowers and herbs.
Praised be You, my Lord,
  through those who give pardon for Your love,
And bear infirmity and tribulation.
Blessed are those who endure in peace
For by You, Most High, shall they be crowned.
Praised by You, my Lord,
  through our Sister Bodily Death,
From whom no one living can escape.
Woe to those who die in mortal sin.
Blessed are those whom death will find
  in Your most holy will,
For the second death shall do them no harm.
Praise and bless my Lord and give Him thanks
And serve Him with great humility.

Francis of Assisi (1225)

The Prayer before the Crucifix

Most High, glorious God,
enlighten the darkness of my heart
and give me true faith,
certain hope,
and perfect charity,
sense and knowledge,
Lord,
That I may carry out
Your holy and true command.
Francis of Assisi (1205/6)

The Earlier Exhortation to the
Brothers and Sisters of Penance

(This is the first version of the Rule of the Secular Franciscan Order.)

In the Name of the Lord!
Those who Do Penance
All those who love the Lord with their whole heart, with their whole soul and mind, with their whole strength and love their neighbours as themselves, who hate their bodies with their vices and sins, who receive the Body and Blood of our Lord Jesus Christ, and who produce worthy fruits of penance. O how happy and blessed are these men and women while they do such things and persevere in doing them, because the Spirit of the Lord will rest upon them and make Its home and

dwelling place among them, and they are children of the heavenly Father Whose works they do, and they are spouses, brothers, and mothers of our Lord Jesus Christ.

We are spouses when the faithful soul is joined by the Holy Spirit to our Lord Jesus Christ. We are brothers to Him when we do the will of the Father who is in heaven. We are mothers when we carry Him in our heart and body through a divine love and a pure and sincere conscience and give birth to Him through a holy activity which must shine as an example before others.

O how glorious it is to have a holy and great Father in heaven! O how holy, consoling to have such a beautiful and wonderful Spouse! O how holy and how loving, gratifying, humbling, peace-giving, sweet, worthy of love, and, above all things, desirable: to have such a Brother and such a Son, our Lord Jesus Christ, Who laid down His life for His sheep and prayed to His Father, saying:

Holy Father, in your name, save those whom you have given me In the world; they were yours and you gave them to me. The words that you gave to me I have given to them, and they accepted them and have believed in truth that I have come from you and they have known that you have sent me.

I pray for them and not for the world. Bless and sanctify them; I sanctify myself for them. I pray not only for them, but for those who will believe in me through their word that they might be sanctified in being one as we are.

I wish, Father, that where I am, they also may be with me that they may see my glory in your kingdom. Amen

Those Who Do Not Do Penance

All those men and women who are not living in penance, who do not receive the Body and Blood of our Lord Jesus Christ, who practice vice and sin and walk after the evil concupiscence and the evil desires of their flesh, who do not observe what they have promised to the Lord, and who in their body serve the world through the desires of the flesh, the concerns of the world and the cares of this life: They are held captive by the devil, whose children they are, and whose works they do. They are blind because they do not see the true light, our Lord Jesus Christ. They do not possess spiritual wisdom because they do not have the Son of God, the true wisdom of the Father. It is said of them: Their wisdom has been swallowed up and cursed are those who turn away from your commands. They see and acknowledge, know and do evil, and knowingly lose their souls.

See, you blind ones, deceived by your enemies: the flesh, the world and the devil, because it is sweet for the body to sin and it is bitter to serve God, for every vice and sin flow and proceed from the human heart as the Lord says in the Gospel. And you have nothing in this world or in that to come. And you think that you will possess this world's vanities for a long time, but you are deceived because a day and an hour will come of which you give no thought, which you do not know, and of which you are unaware when the body becomes weak, death approaches, and it dies a bitter death. And no matter where, when, or how a person dies in the guilt of sin without penance and satisfaction, if he can perform an act of satisfaction and does not do so, the devil snatches his soul from its body with such anguish and distress that no one can know [what it is like] except the one receiving it.

And every talent, ability, knowledge, and wisdom they think they have will be taken away from them. And they leave their wealth to their relatives and friends who take and divide it and afterwards say: "May his soul be cursed because he could have given us more and acquired more than what he distributed to us." Worms eat his body and so body and soul perish in this brief world and they will go to hell where they will be tortured forever.

In the love which is God we beg all those whom these words reach to receive those fragrant words of our Lord Jesus Christ written above with divine love and kindness. And let whoever does not know how to read have them read to them frequently. Because they are spirit and life, they should preserve them together with a holy activity to the end.

And whoever has not done these things will be held accountable before the tribunal of our Lord Jesus Christ on the day of judgment.

Francis of Assisi (1209-1215)

The Praises of God

*(These praises were written in Francis' own hand after
receiving the stigmata)*

You are the holy Lord God Who does wonderful things.
You are strong. You are great. You are the most high.
You are the almighty king. You holy Father,
King of heaven and earth.
You are three and one, the Lord God of gods;
You are the good, all good, the highest good,
Lord God living and true.
You are love, charity; You are wisdom, You are humility,
You are patience, You are beauty, You are meekness,
You are security, You are rest,
You are gladness and joy, You are our hope,
   You are justice,
You are moderation,
   You are all our riches to sufficiency.
You are beauty, You are meekness,
You are the protector,
   You are our custodian and defender,
You are strength, You are refreshment.
   You are our hope,
You are our faith, You are our charity,
You are all our sweetness, You are our eternal life:
Great and wonderful Lord, Almighty God,
   Merciful Saviour.
Francis of Assisi (1224)

A Blessing for Brother Leo

(This blessing was written in Francis' own hand and can be seen in the Capella Della Relique in the Lower Church of the Basilica.)
May the Lord bless you and keep you.
May He show His face to you and be merciful to you.
May He turn His countenance to you and give you peace.
May the Lord bless you, Brother Leo.
Francis of Assisi (1224)

True and Perfect Joy

The same [Brother Leonard] related in the same place that one day at Saint Mary's, blessed Francis called Brother Leo and said: "Brother Leo, write." He responded: "Look, I'm ready!" "Write," he said, "what true joy is."

"A messenger arrives and says that all the Masters of Paris have entered the Order. Write: this isn't true joy! Or, that all the prelates, archbishops and bishops beyond the mountains, as well as the King of France and the King of England [have entered the Order]. Write: this isn't true joy! Again, that my brothers have gone to the non-believers and converted all of them to the faith; again, that I have so much grace from God that I heal the sick and perform many miracles. I tell you true joy doesn't consist in any of these things."

"Then what is true joy?"

"I return from Perugia and arrive here in the dead of night. It's winter time, muddy, and so cold that icicles have formed on the edges of my habit and keep striking my legs and blood flows from such wounds. Freezing, covered with mud and ice, I come to the gate and, after I've knocked and called for some time, a brother comes and asks: 'Who are you?' 'Brother Francis,' I answer. 'Go away!' he says. 'This is not a decent hour to be wandering about! You may not come in!' When I insist, he replies: 'Go away! You are simple and stupid! Don't come back to us again! There are many of us here like you - we don't need you!' I stand again at the door and say: 'For the love of God, take me in tonight!' And he replies: 'I will not! Go to the Crosier's place and ask there!'

"I tell you this: If I had patience and did not become upset, true joy, as well as true virtue and the salvation of my soul, would consist in this."

Francis of Assisi (date unknown)

USEFUL INFORMATION

Assisi provides a range of accommodation and restaurants both for those on a budget and those who like to live in luxury when learning about poverty. The more expensive hotels are described in travel agents and other tourist guides. This book will concentrate on where to stay and eat for those with simpler needs.

Accommodation

There are a number of convents where you can stay but they do need to be booked in advance eg St Anthony's Guest House at Via S. Gabriele dell'Addolorata. They are simple and reasonably inexpensive but often full of large groups of tourists. If you are alone this can be a bit off putting unless you want the company.

The best places to stay for those on a budget are in the Sopra (i.e. the top part of the city). The Albergo La Rocca is a small place to stay, which is typically Italian and is at Via Porto Perlici, 27. For those wanting something simpler than a hotel then there are a number of places advertising 'rooms' ('camere'). Two good examples are a corridor of simple rooms at Ristorante Anfiteatro at the very top of Assisi (Via Anfiteatro Romano, 4. Tel 075/813025) and another corridor of rooms just down the

road run by a charming woman called Maria
(Affitacamere, Alunni Maria Bocchini, Via Dell'
Acquaraio, 3. Tel 075/813182)

There are a few other hotels near Santa Chiara that
are not too expensive, such as the Hotel de Priori and
Hotel Sole.

There is also a campsite outside Assisi where I have
never stayed but friends tell me there is a great
atmosphere with many young people who are discovering
the wonders of Francis.

It is possible to stay outside Assisi but, for short stays,
staying within the walls has advantages. It is much easier
to wander around in the evening and take in the
atmosphere whereas staying in places like Santa Maria
degli Angeli limits this. For those who want a more
peaceful and extended visit to the area then I would
strongly recommend Casa Rosa which has three
beautiful apartments in the hills behind Assisi. It is
managed on site by a friendly English woman. Casa
Rosa is at Santa Maria di Lignano. Tel 075/802322 or
jennifer@casa-rosa.it or *www.casa-rosa.it*

Restaurants

Food and drink are all part of being in Italy. The wine is
of course famously drinkable and light. In the hot
summer, it is even possible to enjoy a refreshing glass
of Italian beer.

The restaurants are varied and there are some which are very smart, and expensive, but which do not look too grand from outside. It is therefore wise to check the price before entering any restaurant. Also, remember that they charge cover (coperto), for your bread, cutlery, tablecloth and service.

As with accommodation, the best places to look for restaurants are in the upper part of the town. I can recommend two. The Trattoria da Erminio is marvellous. It is at Via Montecavallo, 19, which is just above Cattedrale di San Rufino. It is not too busy or too expensive. Try their sausages ('salsicce' in Italian). However, the other restaurant is somewhat different, simpler and is just off Piazza Del Comune. It is called Dal Carro and can be found by going up from Piazza del Comune along Via S. Gabriele Dell' Addolorato where it is on the first snicket to the right - called Vicolo di Nepis. It does great pizzas and has large wooden tables. If you are alone someone else is liable to be put with you at your table. They also have a large log fire to grill meat. Enjoy!

There is one other restaurant worth a mention. It is on the way up to the Carceri at the campsite (Via San Rufino Campagna, 8) and is called Trattoria la Stalla. The locals recommend this place and it is excellent. Again, it is simple, with a log fire and large wooden tables. The food is good enough to tempt Francis himself!

Otherwise, enjoy the little pieces of pizza at lunchtime, the wonderful ice creams and sitting in Piazza Del Comune in the evenings drinking a strong yellow liqueur called 'strega' (which literally means 'witch') or sambuca.

How to get there

Assisi lies between Florence and Rome, near the city of Perugia.

Air

To fly to the area from the UK, a few airports are suitable. Rome is the largest but it is possible to get cheaper flights to Pisa, Bologna or Ancona. Some people fly to Florence but this is a very small airport. Look up the bargain airways.

Road

Assisi is only just off the main A1 motorway, which goes from Rome to Florence. Hiring a car from the airport is a good idea as it gives you the freedom to visit places outside of Assisi.

Rail

Assisi lies on the Foligno-Terontola line. There are through trains from Rome and Florence about every 3 hours otherwise you have to change at either Foligno or

Terontola. The station for Assisi is actually at Santa Maria degli Angeli which is 5 Kilometres away from Assisi.

Hitch hiking

The best way to get to Assisi is to hitch a ride with others. This is the most Franciscan form of travel but is unpredictable and has its dangers.

Travelling around Assisi

There is a regular bus service from the station to Assisi. As with other bus services in Italy you need to buy the ticket before boarding the bus. The station shop sells them. It is a bus that goes to the top of Assisi within the walls and if you only have a short time, it is worth going to the top of Assisi then walking down through the streets to the bottom.

There is no point driving around Assisi. If you have a car, it is best just to park it and walk around. It is useful having a car for visiting places outside Assisi such as Santa Maria Degli Angeli, the Carceri and Monte Subasio.

FURTHER READING

1 Good Books about the life of St Francis

Francis of Assisi by Adrian House (Pimlico, 2001)

St Francis of Assisi by Elizabeth Goudge (currently out of print)

I, Francis by Carlo Carretto (Collins, 1982)

Living the Incarnation by Sr Frances Teresa OSC (Darton, Longman & Todd, 1993)

2 Scholarly books

Francis of Assisi; early documents, volumes I, II and III, (New City Press, 1999)

3 Other Interesting books about St Francis

Muhammed and St Francis by Giulio Basetti-Sani, (S. Francesco-Fiesole, 1975)

In the Steps of St Francis by Ernest Raymond, (Franciscan Herald Press, 1975). This was originally published in 1939 and describes Assisi as it was then

The Icon of the Christ of San Damiano by Marc Picard, (Casa Editrice Franciscans, 1989)

The Small Miracle by Paul Gallico (Amereon Ltd, 1976) - originally published in 1951